RAISING RESILIENT HEARTS

HOW SINGLE FATHERS CAN NURTURE MULTIPLE CHILDREN WITH LOVE AND STRENGTH

CONTENTS

CHAPTER I

Embracing the Role of a Single Father

Understanding the Journey of Single Fatherhood

Being a single father is a unique and challenging journey that many men find themselves navigating. In the book "Raising Resilient Hearts: Single Fathers Nurturing Multiple Children with Love and Strength," we delve into the intricacies of single fatherhood and provide valuable insights and support for those who are in this role.

For single, divorced parents, especially fathers who have been granted custody of their children, the journey of single fatherhood can sometimes feel overwhelming. This subchapter aims to provide guidance and understanding to single fathers as they navigate the various challenges they may encounter along the way.

One of the key aspects we explore is the emotional and mental well-being of single fathers. We recognize that single fathers often face additional pressures and responsibilities, and it is crucial to address their mental health and self-care needs. We offer practical suggestions and resources for single fathers seeking support in this area.

Additionally, we delve into the specific challenges faced by single fathers of school-aged children. Balancing work and parenting responsibilities can be particularly demanding, and we provide tips and strategies for effectively managing these competing priorities. We also discussed the importance of maintaining open communication with teachers and actively participating in their children's education.

Another important topic we cover is single fathers dealing with custody battles. We understand that custody battles can be emotionally draining and highly stressful. We offer guidance on how to navigate the legal system, seek the necessary support, and prioritize the well-being of the children throughout the process.

Lastly, we address the unique circumstances faced by single fathers raising multiple children. From sibling dynamics to managing different personalities and needs, we provide practical advice and techniques to help single fathers create a harmonious and nurturing environment for their children.

"Raising Resilient Hearts: Single Fathers Nurturing Multiple Children with Love and Strength" is a comprehensive guide that caters specifically to the needs of single fathers. It offers support, understanding, and practical strategies to help single fathers navigate their journey with confidence and resilience.

Whether you are a single father seeking guidance on balancing work and parenting responsibilities, dealing with custody battles, or seeking support for mental health and self-care, this book provides the necessary tools and insights to empower you on your journey of single fatherhood.

Navigating The Challenges Of Single Parenthood

Being a single parent can be one of the most rewarding yet challenging experiences in life. For single fathers, managing the responsibilities of raising multiple children alone can feel overwhelming at times. In the subchapter titled "Navigating the Challenges of Single Parenthood" from the book "Raising Resilient Hearts: Single Fathers Nurturing Multiple Children with Love and Strength," we address the unique struggles faced by single fathers and provide guidance and support to help them overcome these obstacles.

Divorce or separation can be a difficult transition for both parents and children. As a single father, coping with the emotional aftermath while fulfilling your parenting duties can seem daunting. This subchapter provides insights and practical strategies to help single fathers cope with the emotional challenges of divorce or separation. It emphasizes the importance of self-care, mental health support, and seeking assistance from friends, family, or support groups.

Single fathers dealing with custody battles often face additional stress and legal complexities. This subchapter offers guidance on navigating the legal system, understanding your rights, and advocating for the well-being of your children. It provides tips on effective communication with your co-parent, fostering a healthy co-parenting relationship, and ensuring the best interests of your children are prioritized.

Balancing work and parenting responsibilities is a common struggle for single fathers. This subchapter explores strategies for managing time effectively, setting boundaries, and seeking support from employers. It discusses the importance of creating a support network, utilizing resources such as childcare services, and finding a work-life balance that allows you to be present for your children while maintaining your professional commitments.

For single fathers of school-aged children, this subchapter delves into the unique challenges they may encounter. It provides guidance on helping children adjust to new routines, managing homework and extracurricular activities, and fostering a positive learning environment at home. It also offers advice on building open lines of communication with your children, addressing any emotional or behavioral issues they may experience, and promoting their overall well-being.

Lastly, this subchapter acknowledges the difficulties of single fathers raising multiple children. It provides practical tips on managing sibling dynamics, promoting harmony and cooperation among siblings, and ensuring each child receives individual attention and support. It emphasizes the importance of fostering a loving and supportive environment where each child's needs are met.

In "Raising Resilient Hearts: Single Fathers Nurturing Multiple Children with Love and Strength," single fathers will find valuable insights, advice, and support to navigate the challenges of single parenthood successfully. Whether you are seeking guidance on co-parenting, mental health support, work-life balance, or managing multiple children, this subchapter provides a comprehensive resource to help you raise resilient children with love and strength.

Embaracing The Rewards Of Single Fatherhood

Introduction:

Being a single father can be an incredibly rewarding and fulfilling experience. While it may come with its fair share of challenges, the rewards that come with single fatherhood are immeasurable. This subchapter aims to explore these rewards and inspire single fathers to embrace their role as nurturers, providers, and role models in their children's lives.

1. Building Strong and Meaningful Relationships:

As a single father, you have the unique opportunity to build strong and meaningful relationships with your children. Being the primary caregiver, you have the chance to forge a deep bond and create lasting memories with your kids. By being actively involved in their lives, you can become their confidant, mentor, and friend.

2. Teaching Life Skills:

Single fathers have the chance to teach their children invaluable life skills. From cooking and cleaning to problem- solving and decision-making, you can empower your children with the knowledge and abilities they need to navigate the world. By imparting these skills, you are setting them up for success in all aspects of their lives.

3. Fostering Resilience:

Single fathers often face unique challenges, such as balancing work and parenting responsibilities or dealing with custody battles. By overcoming these obstacles, you not only demonstrate resilience to your children but also inspire them to be strong and resilient individuals. Your ability to persevere in the face of adversity will teach your children invaluable life lessons.

4. Creating a Supportive Network:

Single fathers seeking support for mental health and self-care can find solace in building a supportive network. Connect with other single fathers, join support groups, or seek professional help when needed. By surrounding yourself with understanding and like-minded individuals, you can share experiences, gain advice, and find comfort in knowing that you are not alone in your journey.

5. Balancing Work and Parenting:

Single fathers often struggle to balance work and parenting responsibilities. However, this challenge can also be a rewarding experience. By effectively managing your time and priorities, you can create a healthy work-life balance. Being present for your children's milestones and achievements will bring immeasurable joy and fulfillment.

Conclusion:

Embracing the rewards of single fatherhood involves recognizing the unique opportunities and experiences that come with the role. By building strong relationships, teaching life skills, fostering resilience, creating a supportive network, and balancing work and parenting responsibilities, single fathers can navigate the challenges with love and strength.

Remember, you are not alone on this journey, and by embracing the rewards, you can raise resilient hearts and create a nurturing environment for your children.

Building A Atrong Foundation Of Your Children

As a single father, navigating the challenges of raising multiple children on your own can feel overwhelming at times. However, by focusing on building a strong foundation for your children, you can provide them with the love, strength, and resilience they need to thrive. In this subchapter, we will explore key strategies and tips that will help you create a solid base for your children's development and well-being.

Primarily, it is crucial to prioritize open communication with your children. By fostering a safe and non-judgmental environment, you can encourage them to express their thoughts, emotions, and concerns. Regular family meetings can provide an opportunity for everyone to share their thoughts and contribute to decision-making, helping your children feel valued and heard.

Another essential aspect of building a strong foundation is setting clear boundaries and expectations. Consistency is key here – establish rules and consequences that are fair and reasonable, and ensure they are consistently applied. This will help your children develop a sense of discipline and responsibility, while also fostering a sense of safety and stability.

In addition to communication and boundaries, it is vital to prioritize your own self-care and mental health. Single fathers often find themselves juggling work and parenting responsibilities, which can lead to burnout. Taking time for yourself – whether it is through engaging in hobbies, seeking support from friends and family, or seeking therapy – is essential to maintain your own well-being. Remember, by prioritizing your own self-care, you are also setting a positive example for your children and teaching them the importance of taking care of themselves.

Finally, seek support and community. Connect with other single fathers who are facing similar challenges. Join support groups or online communities where you can share experiences, seek advice, and learn from others. Building a network of support will not only provide you with valuable insights and guidance but will also help you feel less alone on this journey.

By focusing on building a durable foundation for your children, you are setting them up for success in life. Through open communication, clear boundaries, self-care, and seeking support, you can create a nurturing and resilient environment that will empower your children to thrive despite the challenges they may face. Remember, you are not alone, and with love and strength, you can raise resilient hearts.

Creating A Loving And Supportive Envirenment

As single fathers, we face unique challenges when it comes to raising our children. Whether we are divorced, seeking custody, or simply navigating the complexities of single parenting, it is crucial that we create a loving and supportive environment for our children. In this subchapter, we will explore practical strategies and advice on how to cultivate a nurturing atmosphere that fosters resilience and emotional well-being in our children.

One of the most important aspects of creating a loving environment is establishing open lines of communication with our children. As single fathers, we must make a conscious effort to listen actively and empathetically to our children's thoughts and feelings. By providing a safe space for them to express themselves, we show them that their emotions are valid and valued. Regular family meetings or one-on-one chats can be instrumental in building this foundation of trust and support.

Another essential element in fostering a loving environment is setting clear boundaries and expectations. Children thrive when they have structure and consistency in their lives. As single fathers, it is crucial to establish rules and guidelines that are fair and reasonable. By doing so, we create a sense of security and predictability for our children, which helps them feel loved and supported.

Single fathers often face the challenge of balancing work and parenting responsibilities. It is important to prioritize quality time with our children amidst the demands of our professional lives. By dedicating uninterrupted time to our children, we demonstrate our love and commitment to their well-being. This could involve engaging in shared activities, such as cooking together, playing sports, or simply having heartfelt conversations.

Supporting our own mental health and self-care is also essential in creating a loving environment for our children. As single fathers, we must recognize the importance of taking care of ourselves so that we can be emotionally available for our children. This could involve seeking support through therapy or counseling, joining support groups for single fathers, or engaging in activities that bring us joy and relaxation. By prioritizing our own well-being, we serve as positive role models for our children and create a supportive environment for them to thrive.

Lastly, single fathers raising multiple children face unique challenges. It is crucial to ensure that each child feels loved and valued as an individual. By recognizing and celebrating their unique strengths and talents, we foster a sense of belonging and self-esteem in each child. Additionally, encouraging sibling bonding through shared activities and fostering a sense of teamwork can help create a supportive family dynamic.

In conclusion, creating a loving and supportive environment as single fathers requires intentional effort and commitment. By prioritizing open communication, setting boundaries, balancing work, and parenting responsibilities, supporting our own mental health, and fostering individuality and sibling bonding, we can raise resilient children who thrive despite the challenges they may face. Remember, our role as single fathers is invaluable, and through love and strength, we can create a nurturing environment where our children can flourish.

Establishing Consistency And Structure

As a single father navigating the challenges of parenting multiple children, it is crucial to establish consistency and structure in your household. This subchapter will provide you with valuable insights and practical tips on how to create a stable and nurturing environment for your children, while also maintaining your own well-being.

When it comes to raising resilient hearts, consistency is key. Children thrive in an environment where routines and expectations are clear. Establishing consistent rules and boundaries will help your children feel secure and develop a sense of stability. Consistency also aids in building trust between you and your children, as they learn to rely on you for guidance and support.

Structure is another vital component of a resilient household. Creating a daily routine that includes dedicated time for schoolwork, chores, meals, and leisure activities will help your children develop a sense of order and responsibility. Structure also allows you to manage your time effectively, ensuring that you can balance your work and parenting responsibilities without feeling overwhelmed.

In the context of custody battles, consistency and structure become even more crucial. Children may experience confusion and stress during custody transitions, so it is essential to establish a consistent routine that ensures stability and minimizes disruptions. Communicating openly and honestly with your children about custody arrangements can help ease their anxiety and provide reassurance.

As a single father, it is essential to seek support for your mental health and practice self-care. Building a network of supportive friends, family members, or other single fathers can provide a valuable source of encouragement and advice. Taking time for yourself, engaging in activities that bring you joy, and prioritizing your mental well-being will enable you to be a more present and resilient parent.

Balancing work and parenting responsibilities can be challenging, but establishing consistency and structure can help alleviate some of the stress. Prioritize your time and set realistic expectations for both your work and family life.

Creating a schedule that allows for quality time with your children and ensures that you can meet your professional obligations will promote a healthy work-life balance.

In conclusion, establishing consistency and structure is essential for single fathers raising multiple children. By creating a stable and nurturing environment, you will foster resilience in your children while also taking care of your own well-being. Embrace routines, set clear expectations, seek support, and find balance in your responsibilities as you navigate the rewarding journey of single fatherhood.

CHAPTER 2

Single Fathers of School- Aged Children

Supporting Your Children's Academic Journey

As a single father navigating the challenges of raising multiple children, it is crucial to prioritize and support their academic journey. Education plays a vital role in shaping their future and providing them with the necessary tools to succeed in life. In this subchapter, we will explore various strategies and tips to help you effectively support your children's academic endeavors.

1. Establish a Routine: Consistency is key when it comes to academic success. Create a structured routine that includes set study times, homework sessions, and designated quiet spaces for your children to concentrate on their schoolwork.

2. Communicate with Teachers: Stay actively involved in your children's education by maintaining open lines of communication with their teachers. Attending parent- teacher conferences, reach out via email, and inquire about your child's progress and any areas that may need improvement.

3. Provide a Conducive Learning Environment: Create a peaceful and distraction-free study space at home. Ensure they have access to necessary school supplies, a comfortable desk, and good lighting. Encourage them to personalize their study area and make it an

inviting space.

4. Encourage a Love for Learning: Foster a love for learning by engaging in educational activities outside of school. Take your children to museums, libraries, and cultural events. Encourage reading by setting aside dedicated time for reading and discussing books as a family.

5. Set Realistic Expectations: Every child has unique abilities and strengths. Avoid comparing your children's academic performance to others. Instead, focus on setting realistic goals that encourage personal growth and progress.

6. Seek Additional Support: If your child is struggling academically, consider seeking additional support. This could involve enrolling them in tutoring programs, seeking help from a mentor, or working closely with their teachers to develop an individualized education plan.

7. Teach Time Management: Help your children develop effective time management skills by teaching them how to prioritize tasks, create schedules, and meet deadlines. These skills will not only benefit their academic journey but also prepare them for future responsibilities.

8. Lead by Example: Show your children the importance of education by being a positive role model. Pursue your own learning goals, whether it is taking a course, attending workshops, or furthering your own education. This demonstrates the value you place on knowledge and growth.

In conclusion, supporting your children's academic journey as a single father requires dedication, consistency, and effective communication. By establishing routines, providing a conducive learning environment, fostering a love for learning, and seeking additional support when needed, you can empower your children to excel academically and reach their full potential.

Remember, your involvement and support are invaluable in shaping their educational success and building resilient hearts for a brighter future.

Communication With Teachers And School Staff

As a single father, navigating the complexities of raising multiple children can be challenging enough, but when it comes to dealing with your children's education, it can feel like an entirely different battle. However, effective communication with teachers and school staff is crucial in ensuring your children's academic success and overall well-being. In this subchapter, we will explore strategies and tips to help you establish and maintain positive relationships with the school community.

One of the first steps in effective communication is establishing open lines of communication with your children's teachers.

Attending parent-teacher conferences, introduce yourself, and express your commitment to your children's education. Share pertinent information about your family dynamic and any challenges your children may be facing due to divorce or custody arrangements. This will help teachers better understand your children's needs and tailor their approach accordingly.

Regularly communicating with teachers is vital. Stay informed about your children's progress, assignments, and any upcoming events. Utilize email, phone calls, or even in-person meetings to discuss any concerns or questions you may have. Remember, teachers are there to support your children's learning journey, and by being proactive, you can ensure they are receiving the attention they need.

It is also essential to foster a collaborative relationship with school staff beyond the classroom. Connect with the school counselor or social worker, who can provide valuable emotional support for both you and your children during this transitional period. Seek their guidance on coping strategies, resources for mental health and self-care, and strategies to help your children adjust to the changes in their family structure.

Additionally, consider joining or establishing support groups for single fathers in similar situations. These groups can provide a safe space for sharing experiences, seeking advice, and finding camaraderie. The shared wisdom and support from other single fathers can be invaluable in navigating the challenges of balancing work and parenting responsibilities.

In conclusion, effective communication with teachers and school staff is essential for single fathers raising multiple children. By establishing open lines of communication, staying informed about your children's progress, and fostering collaborative relationships with school staff, you can ensure your children receive the support they need to thrive academically and emotionally. Remember, you are not alone in this journey, and seeking support from both the school community and other single fathers can make a significant difference in your ability to nurture resilient hearts in your children.

Encouraging Learning And Educational Growth

As a single father, one of the most important roles you have is to foster a love for learning and promote educational growth in your children. Whether you are dealing with custody battles, seeking support for mental health and self-care, or balancing work and parenting responsibilities, prioritizing your children's education is crucial. In this subchapter, we will explore effective strategies and practical tips to encourage learning and educational growth in your children.

1. Create a Positive Learning Environment: Establish a dedicated space for studying and completing homework. Ensure it is quiet, well lit, and free from distractions. Encourage your children to take pride in their study area and keep it organized.

2. Set Realistic Goals: Help your children set achievable goals for their education. Break larger goals into smaller, manageable steps, and celebrate their accomplishments along the way. This will instill a sense of motivation and encourage them to continue striving for success.

3. Communicate with Teachers: Establish a strong line of

communication with your children's teachers. Attending parent-teacher conferences, ask about their progress, and discuss any concerns or areas for improvement. Working together with teachers ensures that your children receive the support they need.

4. Foster a Love for Reading: Encourage your children to read by providing them with a wide variety of books and engaging in reading activities together. Set aside regular reading time, visit libraries, and discuss their favorite books to nurture their curiosity and expand their knowledge.

5. Emphasize the Importance of Education: Talk to your children about the value of education and how it can shape their future. Help them understand that learning is a lifelong journey and that their efforts in school will pave the way for a successful and fulfilling life.

6. Be Involved in Homework: Take an active interest in your children's homework. Sit down with them, offer guidance, and assist them when necessary. By showing your support and involvement, you will not only improve their academic performance but also strengthen your bond with them.

7. Encourage Extracurricular Activities: Encourage your children to participate in extracurricular activities that align with their interests and talents. These activities can provide valuable learning experiences, cultivate their passions, and enhance their overall educational growth.

Remember, as a single father, you have the power to shape your children's educational journey. By creating a positive learning environment, setting goals, fostering reading habits, emphasizing the importance of education, being involved in homework, and encouraging extracurricular activities, you will empower your children to thrive academically and reach their full potential. Your dedication and support will not only strengthen their educational growth but also nurture their resilience and set them on a path towards a bright future.

Nurturing Emotional Well-Being In School-Aged Chidren

As single fathers, we understand the importance of fostering emotional well-being in our school-aged children. The formative years of childhood are crucial for building resilience, self-esteem, and emotional intelligence. In this subchapter, we will explore effective strategies to support our children's emotional well-being, enabling them to thrive in various aspects of their lives.

1. Open Communication: Encourage open and honest communication with your children. Create a safe space where they can freely express their thoughts, feelings, and concerns. Be an active listener, validate their emotions, and provide guidance when needed.

2. Establish Routines: Consistency and structure are vital for emotional stability. Establish daily routines that include time for homework, play, family meals, and relaxation. Predictability helps children feel secure and allows them to better manage stress.

3. Encourage Healthy Coping Mechanisms: Teach your children

healthy ways to cope with stress and difficult emotions. Encourage physical activities, creative outlets, and relaxation techniques such as deep breathing or journaling. Help them understand that it is normal to experience various emotions and provide strategies to manage them effectively.

4. Support Social Connections: Foster healthy social connections for your children. Encourage them to build friendships and participate in extracurricular activities. Engage in family activities and outings to strengthen bonds and create a sense of belonging.

5. Teach Emotional Intelligence: Help your children develop emotional intelligence by teaching them to identify, understand, and manage their emotions. Teach them empathy, resilience, and problem-solving skills. Model healthy emotional expression and conflict resolution strategies.

6. Seek Professional Support: If your child is struggling emotionally, do not hesitate to seek professional help. Consult with school counselors, therapists, or psychologists who specialize in child development. They can provide valuable guidance and support for both you and your child.

7. Self-Care: Remember that taking care of your own emotional well-being is crucial for being an effective parent. Prioritize self-care activities such as exercise, hobbies, and spending time with friends. Seek support from other single fathers facing similar challenges through support groups or online communities.

By nurturing emotional well-being in our school-aged children, we equip them with the necessary tools to navigate life's challenges and build resilience. Remember, as single fathers, we have the strength and love to guide our children towards a bright and emotionally healthy future.

Addressing Bullying And Peer Pressure

As a single father raising multiple children, you are aware of the challenges that come with nurturing their emotional well- being. One of the most prevalent issues your children may face is bullying and peer pressure. In this subchapter, we will explore effective strategies to address these concerns and help your children navigate through difficult social situations.

Bullying can have a profound impact on your child's self-esteem and overall mental health. It is essential to create an open and safe environment where your children feel comfortable discussing their experiences with you. Encourage regular communication about their day, their friendships, and any concerns they may have. By fostering trust and active listening, you can gain insight into any potential bullying incidents and take appropriate action.

Teach your children about empathy and kindness from an early age. By instilling these values, they will be more likely to treat others with respect and stand up against bullying. Encourage them to be inclusive and make friends with diverse groups of individuals, helping them to develop a dedicated support network.

Role-play various scenarios with your children, giving them the tools to respond assertively to bullies. Teach them strategies such as using confident body language, speaking up for themselves, and seeking help from a trusted adult. By empowering your children to handle these situations, you are equipping them with the resilience needed to overcome adversity.

In addition to bullying, peer pressure can also be a significant concern for single fathers raising multiple children. Help your children develop a powerful sense of self-identity and values.

Encourage them to make independent decisions based on what they believe is right, rather than succumbing to negative influences. Teach them the importance of setting boundaries and saying no when they feel pressured into doing something against their will.

It is crucial to be actively involved in your children's lives, especially during their formative years. Attend school events, extracurricular activities, and parent-teacher conferences to stay informed about their social interactions. By building a strong relationship with their teachers and peers' parents, you can work together to address any issues that may arise.

Finally, prioritize self-care and mental health for yourself as a single father. Seek support from fellow single fathers or support groups specifically tailored to your needs. Balancing work and parenting responsibilities can be overwhelming but remember that taking care of your own mental well-being enables you to better support your children.

By addressing bullying and peer pressure head-on and providing your children with the necessary tools and support, you are nurturing resilient hearts that will thrive despite life's challenges.

Teaching Resillience And Coping Skills

In today's world, single fathers face unique challenges when it comes to raising multiple children on their own. From juggling work responsibilities to handling custody battles, it's crucial for these fathers to equip themselves with the necessary tools to navigate the ups and downs of parenting. One such tool is teaching resilience and coping skills to both them and their children.

Resilience is the ability to bounce back from demanding situations and overcome adversity. As a single father, you need to not only embody resilience but also teach it to your children. By modeling resilience in your own life, you show your children that setbacks are temporary and that they have the power to overcome any obstacle that comes their way.

One way to teach resilience is by encouraging your children to develop a growth mindset. Help them understand that failures and mistakes are opportunities for growth and learning.

Encourage them to embrace challenges and view them as steppingstones towards success. By fostering a positive and resilient mindset, you are laying the foundation for your children to become strong and resilient individuals.

Coping skills are equally important in helping single fathers and their children navigate the challenges of everyday life. Coping skills are strategies and techniques that individuals use to manage stress, emotions, and tricky situations. By teaching your children effective coping skills, you are equipping them with lifelong tools to handle stress and adversity.

One effective coping skill is practicing self-care. As a single father, it is essential to prioritize your own mental health and well-being. By taking care of yourself, you set an example for your children on the importance of self-care. Encourage your children to engage in activities that bring them joy and help them relax, such as hobbies, exercise, or spending time with loved ones.

Additionally, teaching effective communication skills can help your children express their emotions and needs in a healthy way. Encourage open and honest communication within your family, allowing your children to feel safe and supported in sharing their thoughts and feelings.

In conclusion, teaching resilience and coping skills is vital for single fathers raising multiple children. By instilling resilience in yourself and your children, you empower them to overcome challenges and bounce back from setbacks. Equipping them with coping skills provides them with the tools to manage stress and navigate inconvenient situations. Remember, you are not alone on this journey. Seek support from other single fathers, join support groups, and embrace the power of community.

Together, we can raise resilient hearts and nurture our children with love and strength.

CHAPTER 3

Single Fathers Dealing with Custody Battles

Understanding the Legal Process of Custody Battles

Navigating the legal process of custody battles can be a daunting and challenging experience for single fathers. In this subchapter, we will delve into the essential aspects of the legal system, providing valuable insights and guidance to help single fathers successfully navigate through this difficult terrain.

When it comes to custody battles, knowledge is power. Understanding the legal process is crucial for single fathers seeking custody of their children. This subchapter aims to demystify the legal system, providing a comprehensive overview of the steps involved in custody battles.

We will explore the several types of custody arrangements, including joint custody, sole custody, and visitation rights. It is essential for single fathers to grasp the nuances of each arrangement to make informed decisions that are in the best interest of their children.

Additionally, this subchapter will shed light on the factors that courts consider when determining custody, such as the child's age, their relationship with each parent, and the ability of each parent to provide for the child's physical and emotional needs. By understanding these factors, single fathers can work towards presenting a compelling case that highlights their ability to care for their children.

We will also provide guidance on gathering evidence, preparing for court proceedings, and working with legal professionals. Single fathers will learn about the importance of documenting interactions with their ex-partner, gathering character references, and presenting a solid case in court.

Furthermore, this subchapter will address the emotional toll custody battles can take on single fathers. We will discuss strategies for coping with stress, seeking support for mental health, and practicing self-care. Single fathers will gain insight into maintaining a healthy work-life balance while prioritizing their parenting responsibilities.

For single fathers of multiple children, we will explore effective strategies for managing their unique needs and ensuring their well-being during the custody battle. Practical advice on creating schedules, fostering sibling relationships, and providing emotional support will be provided.

By the end of this subchapter, single fathers will have a comprehensive understanding of the legal process of custody battles and be equipped with the knowledge and tools necessary to navigate this challenging journey. Whether seeking support for mental health, self-care, or balancing work and parenting responsibilities, "Raising Resilient Hearts: Single Fathers Nurturing Multiple Children with

Love and Strength" serves as a valuable resource for single fathers facing the complexities of custody battles.

Seeking Legal Advice And Representation

When navigating the complex world of single fatherhood, it is crucial to understand the importance of seeking legal advice and representation. As a single, divorced parent, you may find yourself facing various challenges, particularly when it comes to custody battles, co-parenting conflicts, and ensuring the well- being of your children. In this subchapter, we will explore the significance of seeking legal guidance and how it can help you navigate the legal system with confidence and resilience.

One of the primary reasons for seeking legal advice is to protect your rights as a father. The custody process can be overwhelming, especially if you are unfamiliar with the legal procedures. An experienced family lawyer can guide you through the legal complexities, ensuring that your rights are upheld and advocating for the best interests of your children. They can help you understand the distinct types of custody arrangements, visitation rights, and child support obligations, empowering you to make informed decisions.

Additionally, seeking legal representation can provide you with the emotional support you need during this challenging time. Custody battles can be emotionally draining, and having a compassionate lawyer by your side can help alleviate some of the stress. They can serve as trusted confidants, offering guidance and reassurance throughout the legal process.

For single fathers dealing with custody battles, it is essential to find a lawyer who specializes in family law and has experience representing fathers. They will understand the unique challenges you face and be equipped to navigate the legal system on your behalf. Look for attorneys who have a track record of success in similar cases, as they will bring invaluable expertise to your situation.

Furthermore, seeking legal advice can also provide you with a sense of empowerment and control over your circumstances. By understanding your legal rights and options, you can actively participate in the decision-making process and work towards securing the best possible outcome for your children.

Remember, seeking legal advice and representation is not a sign of weakness or defeat; rather, it is a proactive step towards ensuring the well-being of your children and protecting your rights as a father. By partnering with a knowledgeable attorney, you can face the challenges of single fatherhood with confidence, resilience, and the legal support you deserve.

Undrestanding Your Rights And Responsibilities

As a single father navigating the challenges of raising multiple children, it is crucial to have a clear understanding of your rights and responsibilities. This subchapter aims to provide you with valuable insights and guidance, ensuring you can confidently face the various aspects of your parenting journey.

Rights and responsibilities go hand in hand and are essential for maintaining a healthy and thriving family dynamic. Knowing your rights empowers you to protect your children's best interests and advocate for their needs. It is equally important to recognize and fulfill your responsibilities as a father, providing your children with the love, support, and stability they need.

One key aspect of understanding your rights is being familiar with custody laws and regulations. Whether you have sole custody or share custody with your ex-partner, knowing the legal framework will enable you to make informed decisions and protect your rights as a parent. Familiarize yourself with the relevant statutes and consult with legal professionals to ensure you are well-informed and prepared.

Alongside your rights, you have a set of responsibilities as a single father. Balancing work and parenting can be challenging, but it is crucial to prioritize your children's well-being. This subchapter will offer strategies and tips to help you manage your time effectively, ensuring you can fulfill your work obligations while actively engaging in your children's lives.

Additionally, self-care and mental health are vital aspects of being a resilient single father. Recognize the importance of taking care of yourself, both physically and emotionally. Seek support networks and resources specifically tailored for single fathers, enabling you to connect with others facing similar challenges and share experiences. Prioritizing your mental health will not only benefit you but also positively impact your children's well-being.

Furthermore, understanding your rights and responsibilities also involves fostering a healthy co-parenting relationship with your ex-partner. Effective communication and cooperation are key in ensuring a positive environment for your children. This subchapter will provide strategies for navigating custody battles and resolving conflicts amicably, focusing on the best interests of your children.

In conclusion, understanding your rights and responsibilities as a single father is crucial for successfully navigating the complexities of raising multiple children. By being well-informed about custody laws, balancing work and parenting responsibilities, prioritizing self-care, and mental health, and fostering a healthy co-parenting relationship, you can create a loving and resilient environment for your children to thrive.

Remember, you are not alone on this journey, and there is support available to help you every step of the way.

Supporting Your Children During Custody Battles

Custody battles can be a challenging and emotionally draining experience for both parents and children involved. As a single father, it is crucial to prioritize the well-being and emotional needs of your children during this challenging time. In this subchapter, we will explore effective strategies for supporting your children through custody battles, ensuring their resilience and emotional stability.

Primarily, open communication is key. Create a safe space for your children to express their feelings, fears, and concerns about the custody battle. Encourage them to share their thoughts without judgment or criticism. By actively listening and validating their emotions, you can provide them with the support they need to navigate through this challenging period.

Maintaining routine and stability is essential. Children thrive on stability, especially during times of uncertainty. Stick to their regular schedules as much as possible and ensure that they have a consistent and secure environment to come home to.

This stability will help them feel safe and grounded amidst the chaos of the custody battle.

Be mindful of your own emotions. It is natural to feel anger, frustration, or sadness during a custody battle. However, it is vital to manage your emotions in a healthy way, as your children are highly perceptive and can easily notice your emotional state. Seek support from friends, family, or even a therapist to help you navigate through your own feelings, allowing you to better support your children.

Encourage healthy coping mechanisms. Help your children develop positive ways to cope with the stress and anxiety they may be experiencing. Encourage them to engage in activities they enjoy, connect with friends and family, or express their emotions through art, writing, or sports. By teaching them effective coping strategies, you are equipping them with lifelong skills to manage stress and adversity.

Lastly, seek professional guidance if necessary. Custody battles can be complex legal processes, and it may be beneficial to consult with a family lawyer who specializes in custody cases. They can provide you with expert advice and guide you through the legal aspects, ensuring the best interests of your children are protected.

Remember, as a single father, you are not alone in this journey. Connect with support groups or online communities for single fathers dealing with custody battles. Sharing experiences, seeking advice, and finding emotional support from others who have gone through similar situations can be immensely beneficial.

By prioritizing the well-being of your children, maintaining open communication, and seeking support when needed, you can support your children through custody battles and help them develop resilience and strength in the face of adversity.

Creating A Safe And Stable Home Environment

As a single father, it is crucial to create a safe and stable home environment for your children. Whether you are divorced or have custody of your children, providing them with a nurturing space is essential for their well-being and development. In this subchapter, we will discuss various strategies and tips to help you build a safe and stable home environment for your children.

1. Establish clear rules and routines: Children thrive in environments with clear expectations and consistent routines. Set rules that are age-appropriate and communicate them effectively to your children. Implement daily routines for meals, homework, and bedtime to provide them with a sense of structure and stability.

2. Create a safe physical space: Ensure that your home is free from hazards and potential dangers. Install safety gates, outlet covers, and secure heavy furniture to prevent accidents. Keep toxic substances out of reach and teach your children about basic safety measures such as not opening the door to strangers.

3. Foster open communication: Encourage your children to express their feelings and concerns openly. Create a safe space where they feel comfortable sharing their thoughts and emotions without fear of judgment or criticism. Listen actively and validate their experiences, showing empathy and understanding.

4. Support mental health and self-care: Single fathers often face unique challenges in balancing work and parenting responsibilities. It is crucial to prioritize your mental health and practice self-care to be emotionally available for your children. Seek support from friends, family, or support groups specifically tailored for single fathers. Take time for yourself to engage in activities that bring you joy and recharge your energy.

5. Encourage sibling bonding: If you are raising multiple children, fostering sibling bonding is important. Encourage them to spend quality time together, engage in activities they all enjoy, and teach them conflict resolution skills. By nurturing a positive sibling relationship, you create a supportive and loving home environment.

6. Seek professional help when needed: If you or your children are facing difficulties that seem beyond your control, do not hesitate to

seek professional help. Reach out to therapists, counselors, or support groups specializing in single fathers and their unique challenges. They can provide guidance and support to navigate through tough times.

Remember, creating a safe and stable home environment is an ongoing process. It requires patience, dedication, and continuous effort. By implementing these strategies, you are providing your children with a solid foundation to grow into resilient individuals who can thrive despite life's challenges.

Communication Openly With Your Children

In the complex and challenging world of single parenting, one of the most vital aspects is maintaining open and honest communication with your children. As a single father, it can be overwhelming to balance your own emotions, work responsibilities, and the needs of multiple children. However, by nurturing open lines of communication, you can create a solid foundation for your family and promote emotional resilience in your children.

When it comes to communicating openly with your children, here are some key strategies to consider:

1. Create a Safe and Supportive Environment: Ensure that your children feel safe and comfortable expressing themselves without fear of judgment or repercussions. Encourage them to share their thoughts, fears, and concerns, and listen attentively to what they have to say.

2. Be Honest and Transparent: Single fathers often face custody battles and other challenging situations. It is essential to be open and honest with your children about these issues, using age-appropriate language. By explaining the situation in a way they can understand, you can help alleviate their anxieties and build trust.

3. Active Listening: Show genuine interest in your children's lives by actively listening to them. This means giving them your undivided attention, maintaining eye contact, and responding thoughtfully. By doing so, you convey the message that their opinions and feelings matter.

4. Foster Emotional Intelligence: Teach your children to identify and express their emotions in healthy ways. Encourage them to talk about their feelings and help them develop coping strategies when facing challenges. By nurturing their emotional intelligence, you equip them with valuable tools for resilience.

5. Encourage Two-Way Communication: Communication is a two-way street. Encourage your children to ask questions, share their thoughts, and engage in discussions. This fosters a sense of mutual respect and strengthens the bond between you and your children.

6. Set Aside Quality Time: In the hustle and bustle of daily life, it can be easy to overlook the importance of quality time. Set aside regular moments to connect with each of your children individually and as a family. This dedicated time will allow for deeper conversations and a stronger emotional connection.

Remember, open communication is an ongoing process that

requires patience and consistency. By prioritizing communication in your single father journey, you are not only providing a safe space for your children but also teaching them valuable skills for their future relationships and emotional well-being.

CHAPTER 4

Single Fathers Seeking Support for Mental Health and Self- Care

Recognizing the Importance of Self-Care

In the chaotic and often overwhelming world of single parenting, it can be easy to overlook the importance of self-care. As a single father, juggling multiple children and the responsibilities that come with custody battles, it is crucial to prioritize your own well-being. In this subchapter, we will explore the significance of self-care for single fathers and provide practical strategies to incorporate it into your daily life.

Being a single father comes with its unique set of challenges, from managing school schedules to dealing with emotional difficulties. It is easy to get caught up in the demands of parenting and forget about taking care of yourself. However, neglecting self-care can lead to burnout, increased stress levels, and decreased resilience.

Recognizing the importance of self-care is the first step towards creating a healthier and more fulfilling life for both you and your children. When you prioritize your well-being, you are better equipped to meet the needs of your children and be emotionally present for them. Remember, you cannot pour from an empty cup.

This subchapter will delve into various aspects of self-care tailored specifically for single fathers. We will discuss the importance of seeking support for mental health and self-care, as well as ways to balance work and parenting responsibilities effectively.

Furthermore, we will explore strategies for managing the stress and emotional toll that custody battles can bring. From practicing mindfulness techniques to engaging in activities that bring you joy and relaxation, we will provide practical tips to help you navigate this challenging process.

Additionally, for single fathers with multiple children, we will delve into strategies for finding balance and maintaining your own physical and emotional health while caring for your children. We will discuss the importance of setting boundaries, seeking assistance from family and friends, and creating a support network.

By recognizing the significance of self-care and implementing strategies to prioritize it, you are not only benefiting yourself but also demonstrating to your children the importance of self- worth and self-care. You are teaching them to value their own well-being and modeling healthy coping mechanisms.

In the following chapters, we will provide practical exercises, real-life examples, and expert advice to support you in your journey towards self-care as a single father. Remember, you deserve to thrive and be resilient, and by taking care of yourself, you are nurturing resilient hearts in your children.

Prioritizing Your Mental And Emotional Well-Being

As a single father, juggling the responsibilities of parenting multiple children can be an overwhelming task. It is easy to get caught up in the daily routine of managing work, household duties, and the needs of your children. However, it is crucial to remember that your mental and emotional well-being should be a top priority. In this subchapter, we will explore the importance of self-care and provide practical strategies for nurturing your mental health.

1. Acknowledge Your Emotions: It is normal to experience a range of emotions while navigating the challenges of single parenthood. Allow yourself to feel these emotions without judgment. Whether it is frustration, sadness, or stress, acknowledging and accepting your emotions is the first step towards prioritizing your mental well-being.

2. Seek Support: Remember, you are not alone on this journey. Reach out to fellow single fathers, join support groups, or seek professional counseling to share your experiences and gain valuable insights. Surrounding yourself with a supportive community can provide a much-needed sense of belonging and understanding.

3. Practice Self-Care: Carving out time for self-care is essential for your overall well-being. Find activities that bring you joy and relaxation, such as reading, exercising, or pursuing hobbies. Set aside dedicated time each day or week for yourself, without feeling guilty about taking a break from your parenting responsibilities.

4. Establish Boundaries: It is important to set boundaries to

maintain a healthy work-life balance. Learn to say no when necessary and prioritize your time effectively. By doing so, you can prevent burnout and ensure that you have enough energy to devote to both your children and you.

5. Develop Coping Strategies: Single fathers dealing with custody battles or other challenging situations may face additional stressors. It is crucial to develop healthy coping mechanisms to manage these difficulties. Consider practices like mindfulness, deep breathing exercises, or journaling to help you navigate through tough times.

6. Communicate with Your Children: Open and honest communication with your children is key to fostering a supportive and understanding relationship. Encourage them to share their feelings and concerns and provide a safe space for them to express themselves. By doing so, you create an environment where everyone's emotional well-being can thrive.

Remember, prioritizing your mental and emotional well-being as a single father is not selfish but rather a necessary step towards being the best parent you can be. By taking care of yourself, you will have the strength, resilience, and love to nurture your children and guide them through life's challenges.

Seeking professional help and support

As a single father navigating the challenges of raising multiple children, it is essential to recognize that you do not have to face these obstacles alone. Seeking professional help and support can be a notable change in your journey towards nurturing resilient hearts in your children. This subchapter will explore various avenues through which you can find the assistance you need to thrive as a single parent.

One of the most crucial forms of support you can seek is professional counseling or therapy. A mental health professional can provide you with a safe space to express your concerns, fears, and frustrations. They can offer guidance on effective parenting strategies, help you develop coping mechanisms, and provide tools to manage stress and anxiety. Additionally, therapy can assist in addressing any unresolved emotional issues stemming from divorce or custody battles, allowing you to heal and move forward.

Furthermore, it is essential to build a network of support around you. Seek out local support groups or online communities specifically tailored for single fathers. These spaces offer the opportunity to connect with others who are facing similar challenges and can provide a sense of camaraderie. Sharing experiences, seeking advice, and receiving encouragement from fellow single fathers can provide immense comfort and reassurance.

When it comes to balancing work and parenting responsibilities, consider exploring resources such as parenting classes or workshops. These programs can equip you with valuable skills and techniques to manage your time effectively, prioritize tasks, and maintain a healthy work-life balance.

Additionally, they may provide insights into effective

communication with co-parents or strategies to handle custody battles.

Finally, do not neglect your own mental health and self-care. It is vital to recognize that taking care of yourself is not selfish but necessary for your well-being and your ability to be present for your children. Seek out professionals who specialize in self-care and mental health for single fathers. They can guide you in developing healthy habits, managing stress, and finding time for self-reflection and rejuvenation.

Remember, seeking professional help and support is not a sign of weakness, but a testament to your dedication as a single father. By investing in your own well-being, you are ensuring that you have the strength and resilience to provide your children with the love and care they deserve.

Establishing A Support Network

In the journey of single fatherhood, one of the most crucial aspects to consider is establishing a fanatical support network. As a single dad, it is essential to recognize that you cannot do it all alone. Building a support system will not only help you navigate the challenges of parenting but also provide you with the emotional and practical support you need. This subchapter aims to guide single, divorced parents, fathers, and those seeking custody, on how to create a robust support network to nurture their multiple children with love and strength.

Being a single father comes with its unique set of challenges, from juggling work responsibilities to ensuring the well-being of your children. Seeking support from like-minded individuals who understand your situation is vital for your mental health and self-care. Connect with other single fathers in your community or join support groups specifically tailored for single fathers. These platforms provide an opportunity to share experiences, seek advice, and offer a sense of camaraderie.

In addition to peer support, it is crucial to cultivate relationships with family and friends who can lend a helping hand when needed. Reach out to relatives, close friends, or even neighbors who can assist with childcare, school pickups, or simply provide a listening ear. By establishing a dedicated support system, you will not only alleviate some of the burdens but also create a network of trusted individuals who can step in when you require assistance.

Balancing work and parenting responsibilities can often feel overwhelming for single fathers. Seek out resources that offer guidance on time management and effective parenting techniques. Online forums, books, and podcasts specifically designed for single fathers of school-aged children can provide valuable insights and practical tips to help you navigate this delicate balance.

Furthermore, prioritizing your mental health and self-care is crucial to your overall well-being. Take the time to invest in activities that bring you joy and relaxation. Whether it is participating in a hobby, engaging in regular exercise, or seeking professional counseling, prioritize self-care to ensure you are mentally and emotionally equipped to handle the challenges that come your way.

Remember, you are not alone on this journey. By establishing a support network, reaching out to other single fathers, and seeking assistance from family and friends, you can create a nurturing environment for your multiple children while also taking care of yourself. Raising resilient hearts requires love, strength, and a team of dedicated individuals who are there to support you every step of the way.

Connection With Other Single Fathers

One of the most important aspects of navigating the challenges of single fatherhood is finding a support system that understands your unique journey. Connecting with other single fathers can provide a valuable source of emotional support, practical advice, and shared experiences. In this subchapter, we will explore the various avenues through which single fathers can connect with others in similar situations, fostering a sense of camaraderie and support.

For single fathers who are new to parenting alone, it can feel isolating and overwhelming. However, reaching out to other single fathers can help alleviate these feelings by providing a safe space to discuss familiar challenges and triumphs. Online communities, such as forums and social media groups, offer a convenient way to connect with other single fathers regardless of geographic location. These platforms allow for 24/7 access to a network of individuals who understand the unique struggles faced by single fathers.

Additionally, many communities have local support groups specifically tailored for single fathers. These groups often organize regular meetings, events, and workshops where single fathers can interact with each other face-to-face. Attending these gatherings can provide an opportunity to form lasting friendships, share resources, and gain valuable insights into successful parenting strategies.

Another avenue for connecting with other single fathers is through parenting organizations and associations. These organizations often offer specialized support for single fathers and can help connect them with mentors or other fathers who have successfully navigated similar challenges. By participating in these programs, single fathers can gain invaluable guidance and reassurance from those who have walked the path before them.

Furthermore, seeking therapy or counseling can also provide an avenue for connecting with other single fathers. Group therapy sessions or support groups specifically designed for single fathers can offer a space for sharing experiences, discussing coping mechanisms, and learning from each other's journeys. These sessions can also address mental health and self-care concerns, offering strategies to manage stress, anxiety, and depression that may arise from the demands of single parenthood.

In conclusion, connecting with other single fathers is crucial for building a dedicated support system and finding solace in a community of individuals who understand the unique challenges of single fatherhood. Whether through online platforms, local support groups, parenting organizations, or therapy sessions, single fathers can find comfort, guidance, and camaraderie from those who have walked a similar path. By reaching out and forming connections with others, single fathers can navigate the difficulties of parenting with greater resilience and strength.

Utilizing Community Rsources For Support

As a single father navigating the challenges of raising multiple children, you may find yourself in need of additional support and resources to help you on this journey. Fortunately, communities offer a wealth of resources that can aid, guidance, and a sense of belonging. In this subchapter, we will explore the various community resources available to single fathers like yourself, providing you with valuable tools to nurture resilient hearts within your family.

One of the first places to turn to for support is local support groups or organizations specifically tailored to the needs of single fathers. These groups can provide a safe space for sharing experiences, exchanging advice, and building a supportive network. Whether you are seeking guidance on custody battles, mental health, self-care, or simply looking for camaraderie with other single fathers, these groups can be an invaluable resource in your journey.

In addition to support groups, community centers often offer a wide range of programs and services designed to assist single parents. From parenting classes and workshops to after-school programs and recreational activities for your children, these centers can help alleviate some of the pressures of balancing work and parenting responsibilities. They also provide an opportunity for your children to socialize and form friendships, fostering their emotional well-being.

Local libraries can be another valuable resource for single fathers. Libraries often host parenting workshops, Storytime sessions, and book clubs that can provide you with insights and ideas on raising resilient children. Furthermore, libraries offer a vast collection of books, both fiction and non-fiction, on a variety of topics related to single parenting, mental health, and self- care. Take advantage of these resources to expand your knowledge and find inspiration.

Lastly, do not overlook the power of online communities and forums. The digital landscape offers a plethora of resources and support networks specifically tailored to the needs of single fathers. Joining online communities can provide you with a sense of belonging, access to valuable advice, and the opportunity to connect with others who share similar experiences.

Remember, as a single father, you do not have to face these challenges alone. By utilizing the community resources available to you, you can find the support, guidance, and strength needed to raise resilient hearts within your family. Embrace these resources and let them empower you on your journey towards nurturing your children with love and strength.

CHAPTER 5

Single Fathers Balancing Work and Parenting Responsibilities

Managing Work-Life Balance

As a single father, managing work-life balance can be a complex and challenging task. Juggling the responsibilities of being a parent, maintaining a career, and taking care of oneself can sometimes feel overwhelming. However, it is crucial to find a healthy equilibrium between work and personal life to ensure the well-being of both you and your children. In this subchapter, we will explore effective strategies for managing work-life balance and provide practical tips to help single fathers navigate this delicate balancing act.

One of the first steps in achieving work-life balance is setting clear boundaries. Establishing specific times for work, family, and personal activities help create a structured routine that benefits both you and your children. Communicate these boundaries with your employer, co-workers, and even your children, so they understand and respect your availability. By setting realistic expectations and boundaries, you can avoid unnecessary stress and feelings of being overwhelmed.

Another essential aspect of work-life balance is self-care. As a single father, it is easy to neglect your own needs while prioritizing your children and work. However, taking care of yourself is crucial for your physical and mental well-being, which in turn enables you to be a better parent. Be available for activities that recharge and rejuvenate you, whether it is exercising, pursuing hobbies, or simply enjoying some quiet time alone. Remember, self-care is not selfish; it is a necessary component of being an effective parent.

Seeking support is also vital in managing work-life balance. Connect with other single fathers who are facing similar challenges. Join support groups or online communities where you can share experiences, seek advice, and find solace in knowing that you are not alone. Additionally, consider reaching out to professionals who can provide guidance on parenting, mental health, and managing stress.

Lastly, it is crucial to prioritize quality time with your children. Although work commitments may sometimes demand your attention, make a conscious effort to be fully present and engaged when you are with your children. Plan activities that allow you to bond and create lasting memories together.

Remember, it is the quality, not the quantity, of time spent with your children that matters most.

In conclusion, managing work-life balance as a single father is a constant challenge, but with the right strategies and mindset, it is achievable. By setting boundaries, practicing self-care, seeking support, and prioritizing quality time with your children, you can create a fulfilling and harmonious life that nurtures both your professional and personal responsibilities.

Remember, you are not alone on this journey, and by taking care of yourself, you are also setting an excellent example for your children to prioritize their own well-being.

Setting Priorities And Boundaries

As a single father, navigating the complexities of raising multiple children can be overwhelming. It is essential to establish clear priorities and boundaries to ensure that you can provide the love and strength your children need while also taking care of yourself. In this subchapter, we will explore effective strategies for setting priorities and boundaries that will help you become a resilient parent.

When it comes to setting priorities, it is crucial to identify what matters most to you and your children. Take the time to reflect on your values and goals as a parent. Consider what you want to prioritize in your children's lives, such as education, emotional well-being, or extracurricular activities. By setting clear priorities, you can make more intentional decisions about how to allocate your time and energy.

In addition to setting priorities, establishing boundaries is equally important. Boundaries help create a sense of stability and structure for both you and your children. Start by defining your personal boundaries and communicating them to your children. This could include setting limits on screen time, establishing consistent bedtimes, or designating specific areas of the house for quiet time or homework.

When co-parenting with an ex-spouse, it is essential to establish boundaries that respect both your needs and the needs of your children. Clearly communicate expectations regarding visitation schedules, parenting responsibilities, and decision-making processes. This will help create a more stable environment for your children and reduce conflicts that may arise during custody battles.

Seeking support for mental health and self-care is another vital aspect of setting boundaries. As a single father, it is easy to neglect your own well-being while focusing on your children. However, taking care of yourself is essential for being the best parent you can be. Look for local support groups, therapists, or online communities that can provide guidance and a safe space for you to share your experiences.

Balancing work and parenting responsibilities can be challenging, but establishing clear boundaries between your professional and personal life is crucial. Set specific working hours and communicate them to your employer and children.

Create a routine that allows you to be present for your children during important moments while also fulfilling your work responsibilities.

Lastly, as a single father of multiple children, it is essential to involve your children in setting priorities and boundaries. This will not only give them a sense of ownership but also teach them valuable skills in decision-making and responsibility.

In conclusion, setting priorities and boundaries is vital for single fathers nurturing multiple children. By identifying your priorities, establishing personal and co-parenting boundaries, seeking support for mental health and self-care, and balancing work and parenting responsibilities, you can create a resilient and loving environment for your children. Remember, by taking care of yourself, you can better care for your children.

Effective Time Management Techniques

As a single father with multiple children, managing your time efficiently is crucial to maintaining a healthy and balanced lifestyle. Juggling the responsibilities of work, parenting, and self-care can be overwhelming, but with the right time management techniques, you can create a harmonious and fulfilling life for you and your children. In this subchapter, we will explore effective time management strategies specifically tailored for single fathers.

1. Prioritize and Plan: Start by identifying your most important tasks and prioritize them accordingly. Create a daily or weekly schedule that outlines your commitments, including work, school activities, appointments, and personal time. By planning ahead, you can ensure that you allocate enough time for each responsibility and avoid feeling overwhelmed.

2. Set Realistic Goals: It is essential to set achievable goals for yourself. Break down larger tasks into smaller, manageable steps. By setting realistic goals, you will feel a sense of accomplishment as you tick off each completed task, boosting your motivation and

productivity.

3. Establish Routines: Consistency is key when it comes to managing your time effectively. Establishing daily routines and sticking to them can help you and your children feel more organized and secure. Set regular bedtimes, mealtimes, and study times to create structure and stability in your household.

4. Delegate and Seek Support: Do not be afraid to ask for help. Single fathers often feel the need to manage everything on their own, but reaching out to family, friends, or support groups can provide much-needed assistance and lighten your load. Delegate tasks to your children based on their age and capabilities, teaching them valuable life skills while easing your own burden.

5. Practice Self-Care: Remember that you cannot pour from an empty cup. Make self-care a priority by scheduling regular time for yourself. Whether it is engaging in a hobby, exercising, or simply relaxing, taking care of your own well-being is essential for your mental and physical health. By prioritizing self-care, you will be better equipped to handle the challenges of single fatherhood.

6. Use Technology Wisely: Utilize technology to your advantage. There are numerous time management apps and tools available that can help you stay organized, set reminders, and track your progress. Use them to streamline your tasks and maximize your efficiency.

By implementing these effective time management techniques, you can create a well-balanced and fulfilling life as a single father.

Remember, it is not about doing everything perfectly; it is about finding a system that works for you and your children. With practice and perseverance, you can create a nurturing and resilient environment that supports the growth and happiness of both you and your children.

Nurturing Relationships With Your Children

As a single father, raising multiple children can be a challenging task. However, building strong and nurturing relationships with your children is essential for their emotional well-being and overall development. In this subchapter, we will explore effective strategies that single fathers can employ to cultivate meaningful connections with their children.

Primarily, open communication is the foundation of any healthy relationship. Take the time to listen to your children, allowing them to express their thoughts, concerns, and feelings. Encourage them to share their experiences, joys, and even their challenges. By actively engaging in conversations, you can create an environment where they feel safe and supported.

Quality time is another crucial aspect of nurturing relationships. Despite the demands of work and other responsibilities, prioritize spending one-on-one time with each of your children. Engage in activities that they enjoy and show genuine interest in their hobbies and passions. Whether it is playing sports, cooking together, or simply having a heartfelt conversation, these moments will foster a sense of belonging and strengthen your bond.

Single fathers often face custody battles, making it important to reassure your children of your love and commitment. Remind them that your presence in their lives remains constant, regardless of the circumstances. Be transparent about any changes or challenges, assuring them that they are not to blame and that they are not alone in facing adversity.

Seeking support for your mental health and practicing self-care is also vital in nurturing relationships with your children. As a single father juggling various responsibilities, it is easy to neglect your own well-being. However, taking care of yourself allows you to be emotionally available and present for your children. Prioritize activities that rejuvenate you, whether it is exercising, meditating, or spending time with friends. Surround yourself with a support system, whether it is through therapy, support groups, or connecting with other single fathers facing similar challenges.

Balancing work and parenting responsibilities can be overwhelming, but creating a routine can help you manage your time effectively. Establishing consistent schedules for meals, homework, playtime, and bedtime will provide structure and stability for your children. This predictability allows them to feel secure and ensures that you have dedicated time for them amidst your other commitments.

In conclusion, nurturing relationships with your children as a single father requires dedication, patience, and open communication. Prioritizing quality time, reinforcing your love and commitment, seeking support for your mental health, and creating a balanced routine are key strategies for fostering strong connections. Remember, by investing in your relationships with your children, you are nurturing resilient hearts that will thrive despite any challenges they may face.

Quality Time And Meaningful Connections

In today's fast-paced and demanding world, finding quality time to spend with our children can often seem like a daunting task. As single fathers, the challenges can be even greater, as we juggle work responsibilities, custody battles, and the daily demands of parenting multiple children. However, it is crucial to prioritize quality time and meaningful connections with our children, as these moments have the power to shape their lives and build resilience.

As single fathers, we may feel overwhelmed and unsure of how to navigate the complexities of parenting alone. But fear not, for this chapter is here to guide and support you on your journey of raising resilient hearts. In this subchapter, we will explore the importance of quality time and how to foster meaningful connections with our children.

Quality time is not about the quantity of hours spent with our children, but rather about the depth of the connection we create during those moments. It is about being fully present, actively listening, and engaging in activities that promote bonding and understanding. Whether it is reading a bedtime story, having a family game night, or simply taking a walk in the park, these small gestures can have a profound impact on our children's emotional well-being.

For single fathers of school-aged children, it is essential to carve out dedicated time for each child individually. This one-on-one time allows us to connect on a deeper level, understand their unique needs, and create a safe space for open communication. By actively involving ourselves in their interests and hobbies, we show our children that we value their individuality and support their passions.

Custody battles can be emotionally draining, but it is crucial to shield our children from the negativity and focus on building a stable and loving environment. Engaging in activities that promote trust and teamwork, such as cooking together or embarking on a weekend adventure, can help strengthen the bond between father and child, despite the challenges faced.

Seeking support for mental health and self-care is vital for single fathers. By prioritizing our own well-being, we are better equipped to show up fully for our children. This subchapter will provide valuable resources and strategies to help single fathers find the support they need and develop self-care routines that nourish their minds, bodies, and spirits.

Lastly, balancing work and parenting responsibilities is a common struggle for single fathers. This subchapter will explore practical tips and strategies to optimize time management, set boundaries, and create a harmonious work-life balance. It will empower single fathers to make the most of the time they have with their children and ensure that these moments are filled with love, joy, and meaningful connections.

Remember, as single fathers, we have the incredible opportunity to shape resilient hearts within our children. By prioritizing quality time and fostering meaningful connections, we can create a sturdy foundation for their emotional well- being and guide them towards a future filled with love, strength, and resilience.

Creating Lasting Memories

As single fathers, we understand the challenges that come with raising multiple children on our own. From juggling work responsibilities to dealing with custody battles, our lives can sometimes feel overwhelming. However, amidst the chaos, it is essential to remember the importance of creating lasting memories with our children. These memories not only strengthen the bond between a father and his children but also provide a sense of stability and resilience for the entire family.

One of the first steps in creating lasting memories is to prioritize quality time with each child individually. We may have multiple children, but each one deserves our undivided attention. Plan special activities that cater to their interests and hobbies.

Whether it is taking a hike, going to a sporting event, or simply having a movie night at home, these one-on-one moments will be cherished for years to come.

Another way to create lasting memories is to involve our children in decision-making. Let them have a say in family activities, vacations, or even the meals they want to cook together. By giving them a sense of ownership, we empower them and create an environment where their voices are heard and valued.

Furthermore, documenting these memories can be a powerful tool. Encourage your children to keep a journal, scrapbook, or even a photo album where they can store their favorite moments. This not only allows them to reminisce about the good times but also provides an opportunity for self-expression and creativity.

Additionally, seek out support networks specifically tailored to single fathers. Join groups or online communities where you can connect with other single dads facing similar challenges. Sharing experiences, advice, and support can help alleviate stress and provide innovative ideas for creating lasting memories with your children.

Lastly, remember to take care of yourself. Balancing work and parenting responsibilities can be exhausting, but it is crucial to prioritize self-care. Set aside time for activities that rejuvenate you, whether it is exercising, reading, or spending time with friends. By taking care of your mental health, you are better equipped to create lasting memories with your children.

In conclusion, as single fathers, we have the unique opportunity to shape the lives of our children and create lasting memories. By prioritizing quality time, involving our children in decision-making, documenting these moments, seeking support networks, and practicing self-care, we can build a solid foundation of resilience and love within our families. These memories will not only bring joy and happiness but will also serve as a reminder of the strength and love that exists within our single father households.

CHAPTER 6

Single Fathers of Multiple Children

Fostering Sibling Relationships

As a single father, one of the most important aspects of nurturing your multiple children is fostering strong sibling relationships. Siblings can provide each other with support, friendship, and a sense of belonging that is crucial for their emotional well-being and resilience. In this subchapter, we will explore effective strategies and practical tips to help you nurture these sibling bonds.

First, it is essential to create a positive and inclusive family environment where each child feels valued and loved.

Encourage open communication and active listening among siblings, ensuring that everyone's voice is heard and respected. By fostering a safe space for sharing thoughts and feelings, you can help your children develop empathy and understanding towards one another.

Another important aspect of fostering sibling relationships is promoting cooperation and teamwork. Encourage your children to engage in shared activities, such as cooking, playing games, or doing household chores together. These collaborative tasks not only foster a sense of unity but also teach valuable life skills and promote a sense of responsibility.

Building a sense of camaraderie among siblings can also be achieved through regular family outings or vacations. These shared experiences create lasting memories and strengthen the bond between siblings. Additionally, consider organizing special sibling-only activities or playdates to allow them to connect on a deeper level.

Conflict is inevitable among siblings, but it is crucial to teach your children effective conflict resolution skills. Encourage them to express their emotions calmly and find mutually agreeable solutions. By mediating conflicts and teaching them the importance of compromise and forgiveness, you can help your children develop healthy ways of resolving disputes.

Lastly, as a single father, it is essential to prioritize each child's individual needs and spend quality one-on-one time with each of them. This will ensure that they feel valued as individuals and not overshadowed by their siblings. Regularly schedule individual outings or special activities where you can bond with each child individually.

By actively fostering sibling relationships, you are providing your children with a lifelong support system. These bonds will not only help them navigate the challenges of childhood but will also serve as a foundation for their future relationships.

Remember, as a single father, you have the power to create a loving and nurturing environment where your children can thrive together.

Encouraging Cooperation And Teamwork

In the journey of single fatherhood, one of the greatest challenges that arise is nurturing a sense of cooperation and teamwork among your children. As a single, divorced parent, it can be overwhelming to handle multiple children on your own. However, by fostering a spirit of collaboration and unity, you can create a harmonious and supportive environment for your family. This subchapter of "Raising Resilient Hearts: Single Fathers Nurturing Multiple Children with Love and Strength" aims to provide valuable insights and practical strategies to help single fathers in fostering cooperation and teamwork among their children.

For single fathers, it is crucial to understand the unique dynamics that arise within a single-parent household. Divorce and custody battles often leave children feeling divided and torn between their parents. Therefore, as a single father, it is essential to establish an open line of communication with your children, encouraging them to express their feelings and concerns. By creating a safe space for them to share their emotions, you can begin to bridge the gaps and build a foundation of trust.

Furthermore, involving your children in decision-making processes can empower them and promote a sense of ownership in family matters. By including them in discussions about routines, chores, and other responsibilities, you can foster a collaborative environment where everyone's opinions and contributions are valued.

Single fathers also face the challenge of balancing work and parenting responsibilities. It is crucial to set aside quality time to engage in activities that promote teamwork and cooperation.

By organizing regular family meetings, where each child can share their achievements, concerns, and ideas, you can encourage a sense of togetherness. Engaging in group activities such as team sports, family game nights, or collaborative projects can also strengthen the bond between siblings and foster a spirit of collaboration.

Additionally, single fathers should seek support for their mental health and self-care. By prioritizing self-care, you can enhance your ability to be present and supportive of your children.

Seeking counseling or joining support groups specifically designed for single fathers can provide invaluable guidance and strategies for promoting cooperation and teamwork.

In conclusion, as a single father, nurturing cooperation and teamwork among your children is vital for a harmonious and supportive family environment. By fostering open communication, involving your children in decision-making, organizing family meetings, and engaging in group activities, you can strengthen the bond between siblings and promote a sense of collaboration. Prioritizing self-care and seeking support are also essential aspects of promoting cooperation and teamwork. Remember, by instilling a cooperative spirit, you are equipping your children with invaluable skills that will benefit them throughout their lives.

Resolving Conflicts And Sibling Rivalry

In the journey of single fatherhood, one of the most challenging aspects can be dealing with conflicts and sibling rivalry among your children. As a single, divorced parent, it is crucial to nurture a loving and harmonious environment for your children to grow and thrive. In this subchapter, we will explore effective strategies to resolve conflicts and foster positive relationships among your children.

Sibling rivalry is a natural phenomenon that occurs in most families. However, for single fathers with multiple children, it can be intensified due to the absence of another parent and the changes that come with divorce or separation. It is essential to acknowledge and address these conflicts promptly to create a peaceful and supportive home.

First, open communication is key. Encourage your children to express their feelings and concerns openly and without judgment. Actively listen to each child's perspective and validate their emotions. By doing so, you are fostering an environment where they feel heard and understood, reducing the need for rivalry.

Teaching conflict resolution skills is also vital. Help your children understand the importance of compromise, empathy, and problem-solving. Encourage them to find mutually beneficial solutions and guide them through the process. By empowering your children to resolve their conflicts independently, they will develop crucial life skills that will serve them well into adulthood.

Another effective strategy is to set clear expectations and boundaries. Establish rules that promote respect, kindness, and cooperation among siblings. Consistently enforce these rules and provide appropriate consequences when necessary. By doing so, you are creating a structured and secure environment where conflicts are less likely to occur.

Furthermore, foster individual relationships with each of your children. Spend quality time with each child individually, engaging in activities they enjoy. This will help them feel valued and loved, reducing the need for rivalry to gain attention or validation.

Lastly, seek support when needed. Being a single father can be overwhelming, and it is important to prioritize your mental health and self-care. Join support groups for single fathers, seek counseling, or connect with other parents who have gone through similar experiences. Remember, you are not alone, and seeking support will strengthen your resilience as a parent.

In conclusion, resolving conflicts and sibling rivalry is essential for single fathers raising multiple children. By implementing open communication, teaching conflict resolution skills, setting clear expectations, fostering individual relationships, and seeking support, you can create a harmonious and loving environment where your children can thrive. Remember, your role as a single father is significant, and by nurturing your children's relationships, you are shaping resilient hearts that will flourish in the face of any challenge.

Manging The Logistics Of Multiple Children

As a single father, managing the organization of multiple children can be a daunting task. From school schedules to extracurricular activities, it may feel like a never-ending juggling act. However, with some strategic planning and a little bit of patience, you can navigate these challenges and create a harmonious routine for your family.

One of the first steps in managing the organization of multiple children is establishing a solid communication system. Whether you are co-parenting or have full custody, it is crucial to keep all parties informed about important dates, events, and changes in schedules. Utilize technology like shared calendars or group chats to ensure everyone is on the same page.

Another essential aspect of managing multiple children is creating a routine that works for your family. This routine should include designated times for homework, meals, and bedtime. Having a consistent schedule will help your children feel more secure and give you a sense of control over your day-to-day responsibilities.

When it comes to extracurricular activities, it is important to set realistic expectations. While it may be tempting to enroll your children in every sport and club available, it is essential to consider your own limitations as a single father. Prioritize activities that align with your family values and your children's interests, and do not be afraid to say no when necessary.

Additionally, seeking support from other single fathers can be incredibly beneficial. Connect with local support groups or online communities where you can share experiences, seek advice, and find solace in knowing that you are not alone in this journey. These support networks can also provide valuable resources and insights on managing the organization of multiple children.

As a single father, it is crucial to prioritize your own mental health and self-care. Balancing work and parenting responsibilities can be overwhelming, but taking care of yourself is essential for your well-being and your ability to care for your children. Find time for activities that recharge you, whether it is going for a run, practicing mindfulness, or spending quality time with friends.

In conclusion, managing the planning of multiple children as a single father may present its challenges, but with strategic planning, open communication, and a supportive network, you can create a harmonious routine for your family. Remember to prioritize your own well-being and seek support when needed. By nurturing your children with love and strength, you are raising resilient hearts and creating a positive environment for their growth and development.

Organizing Schedules And Activities

As a single father, juggling the responsibilities of raising multiple children can feel overwhelming at times. From managing custody battles to balancing work and parenting responsibilities, it is important to find effective strategies for organizing schedules and activities that work for you and your children. In this subchapter, we will explore practical tips and insights to help you navigate the challenges of single fatherhood.

One of the key aspects of organizing schedules and activities is creating a routine that provides structure and stability for your children. Establishing consistent mealtimes, bedtimes, and study hours can help your children feel secure and know what to expect each day. This routine can also help you manage your own time more efficiently, allowing you to allocate specific periods for work, personal time, and quality moments with your children.

Utilizing technology can be a meaningful change when it comes to organizing schedules. There are numerous apps and online tools available that can assist you in managing your family's appointments, school activities, and extracurricular commitments. Consider using shared calendars or scheduling apps that allow you to synchronize your children's schedules with your own, ensuring everyone is on the same page.

In addition to creating a routine and using technology, it is crucial to involve your children in the scheduling process. Encourage them to participate in choosing activities and outings, giving them a sense of ownership and responsibility. This involvement not only helps them develop decision-making skills but also strengthens the bond between you and your children.

As a single father, it is essential to prioritize self-care and mental health. Balancing work and parenting responsibilities can be draining, so make sure to carve out time for yourself. Whether it is practicing mindfulness, engaging in a hobby, or seeking support from other single fathers, taking care of your own well-being will benefit your children as well.

Lastly, do not be afraid to ask for help. Building a support network of other single fathers or seeking professional guidance can provide invaluable assistance in managing your schedules and activities. Remember, you do not have to do it all alone, and seeking support is a sign of strength, not weakness.

In conclusion, organizing schedules and activities as a single father requires careful planning, effective communication, and self-care. By establishing routines, utilizing technology, involving your children, prioritizing self-care, and seeking support, you can create a harmonious and resilient environment for both you and your children. Remember, you are not alone on this journey, and with the right strategies in place, you can navigate the challenges of single fatherhood with love and strength.

Balancing Individual Attention And Family Time

In the journey of single fatherhood, the challenge of striking the right balance between individual attention and family time can often feel overwhelming. As a single, divorced parent, you may find yourself constantly torn between meeting the individual needs of your children and ensuring that quality family time is not compromised. In this subchapter of "Raising Resilient Hearts: Single Fathers Nurturing Multiple Children with Love and Strength," we explore strategies and insights to help you navigate this delicate balance.

For single fathers of school-aged children, it is important to recognize the unique needs of each child. While it may seem challenging to provide individual attention to each child, setting aside dedicated time for one-on-one activities can foster a deeper connection and understanding. Whether it is a special outing, a shared hobby, or even a heartfelt conversation during bedtime, these moments can make a significant impact on your child's emotional well-being.

Dealing with custody battles can further complicate the balancing act. It is crucial to engage in open communication with your ex-partner and establish a co-parenting plan that prioritizes both individual attention and family time. By working together, you can ensure that your children receive the support and attention they need, while also maintaining a healthy relationship with their other parents.

As a single father, seeking support for your mental health and self-care is vital. Taking care of yourself will not only benefit your well-being but also enable you to be more emotionally available for your children. Engaging in activities that replenish your energy, seeking therapy or counseling, and building a network of support can help you navigate the challenges of single fatherhood more efficiently.

Balancing work and parenting responsibilities is another common struggle for single fathers. It is essential to establish clear boundaries and prioritize time with your children. By creating a schedule that allows for dedicated family time, you can ensure that your children feel valued and loved, even amidst your professional commitments.

For single fathers of multiple children, finding moments to connect as a family becomes even more crucial. Encouraging shared activities, such as family game nights or weekend outings, can foster a sense of togetherness and strengthen the sibling bond. Additionally, involving older children in the care and support of their younger siblings can promote a sense of responsibility and teamwork.

In conclusion, balancing individual attention and family time as a single father may be challenging, but with thoughtful planning and open communication, it is possible to create a nurturing environment for your children. By recognizing the unique needs of each child, seeking support for your own well- being, and prioritizing quality family time, you can raise resilient hearts and foster a strong, loving bond with your children.

CHAPTER 7

Facing Challenges and Embracing Resilience

Overcoming Obstacles as a Single Father

Being a single father can be an incredibly challenging and overwhelming journey. From navigating the emotional aftermath of a divorce or separation to balancing work and parenting responsibilities, single fathers often face unique obstacles. However, with love, strength, and resilience, it is possible to overcome these hurdles and raise happy, healthy children. In this subchapter, we will explore various obstacles single fathers may encounter and provide practical strategies for overcoming them.

One of the most common obstacles faced by single fathers is dealing with custody battles. It can be emotionally draining and financially burdensome, but it is essential to stay focused on the best interests of your children. Seek legal advice, document your involvement in your children's lives, and maintain open and respectful communication with your ex-partner.

Another vital aspect to address is supporting your mental health and practicing self-care. Single fathers often neglect their own well-being while focusing on their children's needs. However, taking care of yourself is crucial for maintaining a healthy and nurturing environment for your children. Seek support from friends, family, or support groups specifically designed for single fathers. Be available for activities you enjoy, exercise regularly, and prioritize self-care to recharge and stay resilient.

Balancing work and parenting responsibilities can be particularly challenging for single fathers. It is crucial to establish a routine that allows you to fulfill your professional obligations while still being present and engaged in your children's lives.

Delegate tasks and responsibilities when possible and communicate openly with your employer about your situation to ensure understanding and flexibility.

Additionally, single fathers of multiple children face the added complexity of meeting each child's individual needs. Establish open lines of communication with your children, creating a safe space for them to express their feelings and concerns.

Encourage sibling support and bonding and foster a sense of teamwork within the family unit.

In conclusion, overcoming obstacles as a single father requires resilience, love, and dedication. By seeking support, maintaining self-care, and finding a healthy work-life balance, you can navigate the challenges and raise resilient children. Remember that you are not alone in this journey, and there are resources and communities available to support you. Stay strong, be patient, and cherish the precious moments spent with your children.

Dealing With Financial Pressures

As a single father, you may find yourself facing various financial pressures while nurturing and raising multiple children. The responsibility of providing for your children's needs can be overwhelming, especially when you are the sole breadwinner. However, with the right mindset and strategies, you can navigate these challenges and ensure the well-being of your family.

Primarily, it is essential to create a realistic budget. Take the time to assess your income, expenses, and financial goals.

Prioritize your children's needs and allocate your resources accordingly. Consider seeking professional advice if you need help managing your finances effectively.

Additionally, explore available resources and support systems. Research government assistance programs, grants, or scholarships that could potentially ease your financial burden. Local community centers, non-profit organizations, and churches often offer services and support for single fathers in need. Reach out to these organizations and see how they can help.

To alleviate financial pressures, it is crucial to strike a balance between work and parenting responsibilities. While it may feel tempting to work long hours to secure financial stability, remember that your children also need your presence and attention. Find ways to optimize your work schedule and be available for quality interactions with your children. Consider flexible work arrangements or explore part-time opportunities that allow you to prioritize your children's well-being.

Seeking support for mental health and self-care is equally important. Financial pressures can take a toll on your mental well-being, so it is essential to prioritize self-care activities that help you recharge and de-stress. Engage in activities that bring you joy, such as exercise, hobbies, or spending time with friends. Additionally, consider joining support groups or seeking therapy to share your challenges and feelings with others who can relate.

Remember, you are not alone on this journey. Connect with other single fathers who face similar financial pressures. Share experiences, advice, and resources to support each other.

Building a network of understanding individuals can provide immense emotional support and practical assistance.

Dealing with financial pressures as a single father can be challenging, but with resilience and determination, you can overcome these obstacles. By creating a budget, exploring available resources, balancing work and parenting responsibilities, prioritizing self-care, and seeking support from others, you can navigate these challenges and provide a nurturing environment for your children. Remember, your love and strength as a single father will guide your family through any financial storm that may come your way.

Handling Loneliness And Isolation

Being a single father can be an incredibly rewarding experience, but it can also come with its fair share of challenges, including feelings of loneliness and isolation. Nurturing multiple children on your own requires immense strength, but it is important to remember that you do not have to face these difficulties alone. This subchapter of "Raising Resilient Hearts: Single Fathers Nurturing Multiple Children with Love and Strength" is dedicated to helping single, divorced parents, specifically fathers, navigate the often overwhelming emotions of loneliness and isolation.

Loneliness can creep in when you least expect it, especially during the quiet moments when the children are asleep or away. It is essential to recognize that these feelings are normal and that you are not alone in experiencing them. Reach out to other single fathers in your community or join support groups specifically designed for single parents. Connecting with individuals who share similar experiences can provide a support system that understands your unique challenges and can offer valuable advice and companionship.

Isolation can also be a result of custody battles or the demands of balancing work and parenting responsibilities. It is crucial to prioritize self-care and mental well-being, as neglecting your own needs can intensify feelings of isolation. Take time for yourself, whether it is through hobbies, exercise, or simply enjoying moments of solitude. Remember, taking care of yourself is not selfish but rather an essential part of being a good father to your children.

In addition to seeking support from others, finding ways to create meaningful connections with your children is vital. Plan regular activities or outings that allow you to bond with your kids and build lasting memories. Engaging in open and honest communication with your children can also help alleviate feelings of loneliness and isolation. Encourage them to express their emotions and share their thoughts, fostering an environment of trust and understanding.

Remember, being a single father is a journey that requires resilience and strength. Embrace the challenges and seek support when needed. By prioritizing self-care, establishing connections with others, and nurturing a strong bond with your children, you can overcome feelings of loneliness and isolation and create a supportive and loving environment for your family.

In conclusion, this subchapter provides guidance and support for single fathers who may be struggling with loneliness and isolation. By acknowledging these feelings as normal and seeking support from others, prioritizing self-care, and fostering meaningful connections with your children, you can navigate the challenges of single parenthood with love and strength.

Remember, you are not alone on this journey, and there are resources available to help you every step of the way.

Cultivating Resiliance In Your Children

As a single father, raising multiple children can be a challenging and demanding task, especially after going through a divorce or custody battle. However, it is crucial to focus on nurturing resilience in your children to help them navigate through life's difficulties. In the subchapter "Cultivating Resilience in Your Children," we will explore strategies and techniques that single fathers can employ to foster resilience in their school- aged children.

Resilience is the ability to bounce back from adversity and adapt to challenging circumstances. It is an essential skill that can enable your children to cope with the changes and uncertainties that come with divorce or separation. By developing resilience, your children will grow into strong, confident individuals who can overcome obstacles and thrive in life.

One of the most effective ways to cultivate resilience in your children is to provide them with a stable and supportive environment. As a single father, it is important to establish routines and consistent rules that create a sense of structure and security. This stability can help your children feel safe and develop a sense of control over their lives.

Open and honest communication is another key component of resilience-building. Encourage your children to express their feelings and thoughts and listen to them without judgment. Validate their emotions and let them know that it is okay to experience a range of feelings during this challenging time. By fostering open communication, you are teaching them healthy coping mechanisms and helping them build emotional resilience.

Additionally, teach your children problem-solving and decision-making skills. Encourage them to think critically, explore different options, and make choices independently. By empowering them to solve their own problems, you are instilling a sense of resilience and self-confidence that will serve them well throughout their lives.

As a single father, it is also vital to prioritize your own mental health and self-care. By taking care of yourself, you can model resilience for your children and show them the importance of self-care. Seek support from friends, family, or support groups specifically designed for single fathers. Balancing work and parenting responsibilities can be overwhelming, but by seeking assistance and practicing self-care, you can better support your children's resilience.

In conclusion, "Cultivating Resilience in Your Children" is a crucial subchapter for single fathers raising multiple children. By establishing stability, fostering open communication, teaching problem-solving skills, and prioritizing self-care, you can help your children develop the resilience needed to navigate the challenges they may face. Remember, you are not alone on this journey as there are numerous support systems available for single fathers seeking guidance and support.

Together, we can raise resilient hearts and empower our children to thrive.

Teaching Problem-Solving Skills

As a single father dealing with the challenges of raising multiple children, it is crucial to equip yourself with effective problem-solving skills. Nurturing resilient hearts in your children requires you to not only provide love and strength but also teach them how to navigate life's obstacles. By instilling problem-solving skills in your children, you are empowering them to face challenges head-on and develop the resilience they need to thrive.

One of the first steps in teaching problem-solving skills is to model it yourself. Children learn by observing their parents, so it is essential to demonstrate effective problem-solving techniques in your own life. Whether you are dealing with a custody battle or trying to balance work and parenting responsibilities, show your children how you approach these challenges with a positive mindset and determination.

Encourage open communication with your children. Create a safe space where they feel comfortable sharing their problems and concerns with you. By actively listening to their issues, you can guide them in finding solutions. Teach them to break down problems into smaller, more manageable parts and brainstorm potential solutions together. This collaborative approach not only fosters critical thinking skills but also strengthens the bond between you and your children.

Another valuable technique is to encourage creativity and critical thinking. Encourage your children to think freely and explore different perspectives when facing a problem. Engage them in discussions that promote critical thinking and help them analyze situations from various angles. By nurturing their creativity, you are instilling a valuable problem-solving skill that can be applied to any situation.

Teaching problem-solving skills also involves teaching resilience. Help your children understand that setbacks and failures are a natural part of life. Emphasize the importance of perseverance and resilience in the face of challenges. Teach them to view setbacks as learning opportunities and encourage them to bounce back stronger. By fostering resilience, you are equipping your children with the mental strength they need to overcome any obstacle.

Lastly, seek support for yourself as a single father. Join support groups or seek therapy to ensure your mental health and self- care needs are met. Taking care of yourself is essential in providing the guidance and support your children require.

In conclusion, teaching problem-solving skills is crucial for single fathers raising multiple children. By modeling effective problem-solving techniques, fostering open communication, encouraging creativity and critical thinking, and nurturing resilience, you are equipping your children with the tools they need to navigate life's challenges successfully. Remember to

seek support for yourself as well, as your well-being is vital in being the best father you can be.

Encouraging A Growth Mindset

In the journey of single fatherhood, one of the most valuable tools we can equip ourselves with is a growth mindset. This mindset is not only beneficial for our own personal development, but also for nurturing our children's resilience and fostering their ability to overcome challenges. In this subchapter, we will explore the concept of a growth mindset and how we can encourage its growth within ourselves and our children.

A growth mindset is the belief that our abilities and intelligence can be developed through effort, learning, and persistence. It is the understanding that failure and setbacks are not permanent, but rather opportunities for growth and learning. As single fathers navigating the complexities of parenting, custody battles, and multiple children, cultivating a growth mindset is crucial for our own well-being and our ability to provide the support our children need.

First and foremost, it is important for us to model a growth mindset ourselves. Our children look up to us as role models, and by demonstrating a positive attitude towards challenges and setbacks, we inspire them to do the same. We can openly share our own struggles and emphasize the importance of perseverance and a willingness to learn from mistakes.

Additionally, we can create an environment that fosters a growth mindset. Encouraging our children to take on new challenges, set goals, and embrace the learning process will help them develop a growth mindset. Praising their effort and determination rather than solely focusing on outcomes will reinforce the idea that their abilities can be developed.

It is also crucial to support our children's mental health and self-care. Teaching them the importance of self-compassion, self-reflection, and resilience will help them navigate the ups and downs of life. Encouraging activities such as journaling, mindfulness, and seeking professional help when needed can further strengthen their mental well-being.

Lastly, as single fathers balance work and parenting responsibilities, it is essential to prioritize self-care. Taking care of ourselves physically, mentally, and emotionally allows us to be better equipped to support our children. Seeking support from fellow single fathers, joining support groups, and practicing self-compassion are all ways to prioritize our own well-being.

In conclusion, cultivating a growth mindset within us and our children is a powerful tool in navigating the challenges of single fatherhood. By modeling a growth mindset, creating an environment that fosters it, prioritizing mental health and self-care, we can raise resilient children who are equipped to face the world with strength and determination. Remember, the journey of single fatherhood is not without its hurdles, but with a growth mindset, we can overcome them and raise resilient hearts.

CHAPTER 8

Celebrating Your Journey as a Single Father

Reflecting on Your Accomplishments

As a single father, it is essential to take a moment to reflect on your accomplishments. During the chaos and challenges that come with raising multiple children on your own, it is easy to overlook the progress you have made and the hurdles you have overcome. However, acknowledging and celebrating your achievements is crucial for both your mental well-being and your children's.

One of the first accomplishments to recognize is the strength and resilience you have shown in taking on the role of a single father. It takes immense courage and determination to navigate the complexities of parenting alone, especially when dealing with the aftermath of a divorce or custody battle. By acknowledging your ability to provide love, support, and stability to your children, you reinforce your belief in your own capabilities.

Another accomplishment to reflect on is the bond you have developed with your children. Being a single father means taking on multiple roles and responsibilities, including being a nurturer, provider, and role model. The fact that you have managed to foster a strong connection with your children while juggling these various duties is a testament to your dedication and love.

Balancing work and parenting responsibilities is a constant challenge for single fathers. It is important to recognize the accomplishments you have made in finding a way to manage both aspects of your life. Whether it is through effective time management, seeking support from friends and family, or making necessary adjustments to your schedule, applaud yourself for finding a work-life balance that allows you to be present for your children while also meeting your professional obligations.

Additionally, it is vital to acknowledge the steps you have taken to prioritize your mental health and self-care. Being a single father can be emotionally and physically draining, and it is crucial to be available for yourself. Celebrate the moments when you have sought support, whether through therapy, support groups, or engaging in activities that bring you joy and relaxation. Taking care of your own well-being enables you to better care for your children.

In conclusion, reflecting on your accomplishments as a single father is an empowering exercise that can boost your self- esteem and reinforce your commitment to your children's well- being. By acknowledging your strength, resilience, and ability to balance various responsibilities, you set a positive example for your children and inspire other single fathers facing similar challenges. Remember, you are doing an incredible job, and your accomplishments deserve recognition and celebration.

Recognizing Your Strengths And Growth

As a single father navigating the challenges of raising multiple children, it is crucial to recognize and embrace your strengths and personal growth. In the journey of parenthood, especially for divorced or single parents, acknowledging your own abilities and progress can significantly impact your resilience and ability to provide love and strength to your children. In this subchapter, we will explore various aspects of recognizing your strengths and growth as a single father, offering support and guidance specific to your situation.

For single fathers of school-aged children, you are facing the unique task of balancing their educational needs with your own responsibilities. It is essential to acknowledge your ability to provide structure, support, and encouragement in their academic journey. Recognize the progress your children have made under your guidance and celebrate their achievements, no matter how small. By acknowledging your strengths as an educator, mentor, and provider, you can instill confidence and resilience in your children.

Single fathers dealing with custody battles often face immense emotional and psychological challenges. It is crucial to recognize your strength in advocating for your children's well- being and fighting for their best interests. Embrace the growth you have achieved in navigating the complexities of the legal system and seek support from other single fathers who have faced similar struggles. Recognizing your resilience and determination will inspire your children and help them feel secure amidst the turmoil.

Self-care and mental health are vital for single fathers seeking support and balance. Recognize the strength it takes to prioritize your well-being alongside your parenting responsibilities. Embrace the growth you have achieved in seeking professional help or engaging in activities that bring you joy and rejuvenation. By practicing self-care, you become a role model for your children, teaching them the importance of self-love and resilience.

Balancing work and parenting responsibilities is no easy task for single fathers. Recognize your strength in juggling multiple roles and responsibilities. Acknowledge the growth you have experienced in managing your time efficiently and setting boundaries to ensure quality time with your children. Seek support from fellow single fathers who have successfully navigated similar challenges, learning from their experiences and insights.

Lastly, single fathers raising multiple children must recognize their strength in creating a nurturing and loving environment. Embrace the growth you have achieved in fostering sibling relationships, teaching cooperation, and nurturing individual personalities. Celebrate the small triumphs and milestones your children reach, acknowledging the impact of your love and dedication in their lives.

In conclusion, recognizing your strengths and personal growth as a single father is essential for raising resilient children. By acknowledging your abilities, seeking support, and celebrating your progress, you can provide love and strength to your children while nurturing your own well-being. Remember that you are not alone in this journey, and there are resources and communities available to support you. Embrace your strengths and growth and continue to be the loving and resilient parent your children need.

Embaracing Fatherhood With Gratitude

Introduction:

Becoming a single father can be a daunting and overwhelming experience. The challenges of raising multiple children on your own, while juggling work and personal responsibilities, can often leave you feeling exhausted and discouraged. However, amid these trials, it is crucial to embrace fatherhood with gratitude. This subchapter of "Raising Resilient Hearts: Single Fathers Nurturing Multiple Children with Love and Strength" explores the importance of gratitude and offers practical strategies to help single fathers navigate the complexities of parenting with a positive mindset.

1. The Power of Gratitude:

Gratitude is a transformative tool that can enhance your overall well-being and positively impact your parenting journey. By cultivating a grateful mindset, you can shift your focus from the challenges to the blessings in your life. Expressing gratitude not only improves your mental health but also strengthens your connection with your children.

2. Finding Silver Linings:

Being a single father may not have been part of your original plan, but it presents unique opportunities for growth and bonding with your children. Take the time to identify the positive aspects in your situation, such as the chance to build a deeper relationship with your kids or the freedom to create your own parenting style.

3. Practicing Self-Care:

As a single father, it is essential to prioritize your mental health and well-being. Incorporate self-care practices into your routine, such as exercise, meditation, or engaging in hobbies you enjoy. By taking care of yourself, you will be better equipped to handle the challenges of fatherhood and provide the support your children need.

4. Seeking Support:

No father should have to face the journey of single parenthood alone. Seek out support networks specifically designed for single fathers, where you can connect with like-minded individuals who understand your unique circumstances. These communities can provide a safe space for sharing experiences, seeking advice, and finding emotional support.

5. Gratitude Rituals:

Integrate gratitude into your daily life by establishing simple rituals with your children. Encourage them to express gratitude through journaling, creating gratitude jars, or sharing three things they are grateful for each day. These practices will not only foster a positive mindset but also strengthen the bond between you and your children.

Conclusion:

Embracing fatherhood with gratitude is a powerful mindset that can transform your experience as a single father. By focusing on the positives, practicing self-care, seeking support, and integrating gratitude rituals, you can navigate the challenges of single parenthood with love, strength, and resilience. Remember, you are not alone in this journey, and your children are fortunate to have a dedicated, loving father like you.

Looking Ahead To A Bright Future

As single fathers, we face unique challenges and responsibilities in raising and nurturing our children. Whether we are divorced, have custody battles, or are simply seeking support for mental health and self-care, it is crucial to remember that our journey does not end here. In fact, it is just the beginning of a bright future for both us and our children.

Being a single father of school-aged children means juggling multiple roles, from being a provider to a caregiver, mentor, and friend. It can be overwhelming at times, but it is essential to stay positive and focused on the future we want to create for our kids.

One of the key aspects of looking ahead to a bright future is seeking support. We do not have to face these challenges alone.

Connecting with other single fathers who are going through similar experiences can provide a valuable network of support and understanding. Whether through local support groups or online communities, reaching out and sharing our stories can help us navigate the difficulties of single parenting.

Moreover, taking care of our mental health and practicing self- care is vital in ensuring a bright future for ourselves and our children. As single fathers, it is easy to neglect our own well- being while focusing solely on our children's needs. However, by prioritizing self- care, we become better equipped to support and guide our children effectively. Whether it is setting aside time for hobbies, exercise, or seeking professional help when needed, taking care of us is not a luxury but a necessity.

Balancing work and parenting responsibilities is another challenge that single fathers face. It is important to find a healthy equilibrium between the two, ensuring that we are present and engaged in our children's lives while also meeting our professional obligations. Setting boundaries, seeking flexible work arrangements, and involving our children in our daily routines can help create a harmonious balance between work and family life.

Lastly, for single fathers with multiple children, it is essential to foster a sense of unity and love within the family. Encouraging open communication, creating shared experiences, and celebrating individual achievements can help strengthen the bond between siblings and provide a stable foundation for their growth and development.

In conclusion, as single fathers, we have the power to shape a bright future for ourselves and our children. By seeking support, prioritizing mental health and self-care, balancing work, and parenting responsibilities, and fostering unity within our families, we can navigate the challenges of single parenting with strength and resilience. Remember, the road may be long, but the future is bright, and together, we can raise resilient hearts.

Setting Goals For Yourself And Your Children

As a single father, raising multiple children on your own can be a challenging task. Balancing work and parenting responsibilities, dealing with custody battles, and seeking support for mental health and self-care can feel overwhelming at times. However, by setting goals for yourself and your children, you can create a roadmap for success and cultivate resilience within your family.

Setting goals is crucial for personal growth and development. It allows you to have a clear direction and purpose in life. When it comes to parenting, setting goals for your children is equally important. By providing them with a sense of purpose and direction, you can empower them to overcome obstacles and thrive in life.

Start by setting short-term and long-term goals for yourself. Short-term goals could include dedicating a specific amount of quality time to each child every day or setting aside regular time for self-care activities such as exercise or hobbies. Long- term goals may involve career advancement or financial stability. Write these goals down and create a plan to achieve them. Breaking them down into manageable steps will make them more attainable.

When setting goals for your children, involve them in the process. This will give them a sense of ownership and responsibility. Encourage them to dream big and think about what they want to achieve in various aspects of their lives, such as academics, extracurricular activities, or personal growth. Help them break these goals down into smaller, achievable steps, and create a timeline for them to follow.

Remember to celebrate milestones and achievements along the way. This will not only boost your children's self-esteem but also reinforce the importance of setting and reaching goals.

Encourage them to reflect on their progress regularly and make adjustments if needed.

In addition to personal and academic goals, focus on fostering resilience in your children. Teach them the importance of perseverance, adaptability, and problem-solving skills. Help them understand that setbacks and failures are part of life but can be valuable learning experiences.

Lastly, seek support from your community and other single fathers. Connect with support groups or online forums where you can share experiences, seek advice, and find solace.

Remember, you are not alone in this journey, and by supporting each other, you can navigate the challenges of single fatherhood more effectively.

In conclusion, setting goals for yourself and your children is essential for single fathers raising multiple children. By providing a sense of purpose and direction, you can cultivate resilience within your family and empower your children to thrive. Remember to involve your children in the goal-setting process, celebrate achievements, and seek support from your community. With determination and support, you can create a nurturing and resilient environment for yourself and your children.

Embracing Optimism And Hope

In the journey of single parenthood, it is all too easy to become overwhelmed by the challenges and responsibilities that lie ahead. As a single father, navigating the complexities of raising multiple children can often feel like an uphill battle. However, it is crucial to remember that within every struggle lies an opportunity for growth and transformation. By embracing optimism and hope, you can cultivate resilience within yourself and your children, paving the way for a brighter future.

One of the first steps in embracing optimism and hope is to shift your mindset. Instead of dwelling on the difficulties that come with being a single father, focus on the strengths and capabilities that you possess. Recognize that you have the power to overcome any obstacles that come your way, and that your love and dedication to your children will guide you through even the toughest times.

Another important aspect of embracing optimism and hope is seeking support. As a single father, it is essential to build a network of like-minded individuals who understand the unique challenges you face. Connect with other single fathers through support groups or online communities, where you can share your experiences, seek advice, and offer support to others who may be going through similar situations. Surrounding yourself with positive influences will not only provide you with a sense of belonging but also remind you that you are not alone in your journey.

Maintaining a healthy mindset goes hand in hand with self- care. It is crucial to prioritize your mental health and well-being. Be available for activities that bring you joy and help you recharge, whether it is exercising, meditating, or pursuing hobbies. Taking care of yourself will not only benefit you but also enable you to be the best possible father to your children.

Lastly, keep in mind that your children are watching and learning from your actions. By embracing optimism and hope, you are setting an example for them to follow. Teach them the importance of resilience, perseverance, and a positive outlook on life. Encourage them to dream big and believe in their abilities to overcome any challenges they may face.

In conclusion, as a single father, it is essential to embrace optimism and hope to navigate the complexities of parenthood successfully. By shifting your mindset, seeking support, practicing self-care, and setting a positive example for your children, you can cultivate resilience and create a nurturing environment where they can thrive. Remember, even in the face of adversity, hope is a powerful force that can transform your life and the lives of your children.

www.ingramcontent.com/pod-product-compliance
Lightning Source LLC
Chambersburg PA
CBHW072027150726
47999CB00002B/786